TiVo

ABDO
Publishing Company

TECHNOLOGY
PIONEERS

TiVo

THE COMPANY AND ITS FOUNDERS

by Kristine Carlson Asselin

Content Consultant
Chris Morris
Freelance Journalist, Technology Specialist
www.chrismorrisjournalist.com

CREDITS

Published by ABDO Publishing Company, PO Box 398166, Minneapolis, MN 55439. Copyright © 2013 by Abdo Consulting Group, Inc. International copyrights reserved in all countries. No part of this book may be reproduced in any form without written permission from the publisher. The Essential Library™ is a trademark and logo of ABDO Publishing Company.

Printed in the United States of America,
North Mankato, Minnesota
062012
092012

Editor: Rebecca Felix
Series Designer: Emily Love

Library of Congress Cataloging-in-Publication Data
Asselin, Kristine Carlson.
  TiVo : the company and its founders / Kristine Carlson Asselin.
    p. cm. -- (Tech pioneers)
  Includes bibliographical references and index.
  ISBN 978-1-61783-336-6 (alk. paper)
  1. Ramsay, Mike, 1950---Juvenile literature. 2. Barton, Jim, 1958---Juvenile literature. 3. Electrical engineers--Great Britain--Biography. 4. Electrical engineers--United States--Biography. 5. Digital video recorders--Juvenile literature. I. Title.
  TK6655.D54A87 2013
  338.7'62138833--dc23
                                    2012011531

TABLE OF CONTENTS

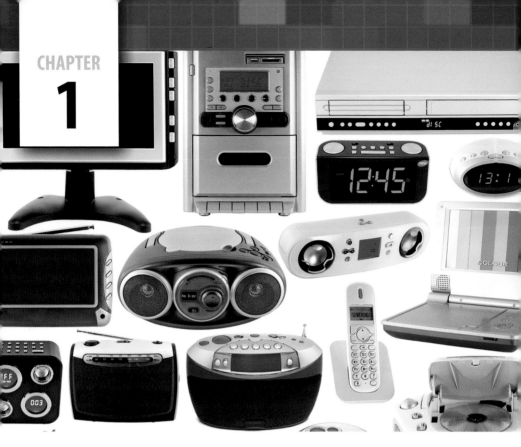

Mike Ramsay and Jim Barton envisioned their home network
managing all types of digital home data.

AN IDEA FORMS

Mike Ramsay and Jim Barton did not set out to change the future of commercial television. When they met in the 1980s, both were hardworking executives at Hewlett Packard (HP), a large, established technology corporation. They were colleagues at a different technology company, Silicon Graphics Inc. (SGI), in the early 1990s.

One day in the late spring or early summer of 1997, Ramsay and Barton met for lunch. Ramsay had just quit SGI that May, and Barton had left a year before. Over lunch, they discussed Barton's new start-up company, Network Age Software, their past work experiences together, and their families and mutual friends.

The seed of an idea was also born during this lunch. Ramsay and Barton realized they would make good partners and decided to join forces. They envisioned creating a product that would allow people to manage many different types of technology in their homes. This "smart house" concept connected all the appliances in the home to a computer and Internet access.[1] The homeowner

SILICON GRAPHICS

SGI was best known for creating special effects software used in movies. Special effects software gives filmmakers a way to create special or fantasy scenes that are realistic looking and would be impossible to duplicate any other way. SGI's partners included visual effects company Industrial Light & Magic and Pixar Animation Studios, two of the most influential users of special effects software in the industry in the 1990s and 2000s. Two of SGI's most successful projects using special effects software were the dinosaurs in the 1993 film *Jurassic Park* and the tornadoes in *Twister* in 1996.

could manage all devices that could be controlled by manipulating digital data, such as photos, voice mail, music storage and playback, and television. The system would even control the coffeemaker and tell the homeowner when the milk in the refrigerator went sour. Their company, Teleworld Inc., was incorporated on August 4, 1997.

However, as they set to work making their vision come to life, Ramsay and Barton discovered that their home network concept was difficult for the average consumer to understand. Most consumers just could not envision the need for a system that did things such as control the thermostat from their office chair or automatically order groceries. Furthermore, the technology was not yet available that could handle all the different systems needed for their design to work. Ramsay and Barton went back to the drawing board to determine the course of their company.

Instead of scrapping their original idea completely, they settled on one component of the home networking system they thought they could successfully achieve: giving consumers the ability to record and pause live television. The idea was groundbreaking and Ramsay and Barton understood the technology and had the knowledge to make it happen. Plus, this scaled-back concept of their idea was a lot easier to describe to customers. Everyone in their test markets liked the idea of more personal control of what they watched on television. The product, as Barton and Ramsay put it, would let "you watch anything you want to watch when you want to watch it."[2]

PERSONAL TELEVISION RECEIVER

The duo called their invention a personal television receiver. But it would come to be known as either a PVR (personal video recorder) or DVR (digital video recorder), the latter being the most commonly used term. It was a black box, a lot like a cable box, with a hard drive, or memory. The DVR recorded programming, but not in the way its clunky ancestor, the videocassette recorder (VCR), did.

THE FIRST VCR

Video recorders were first introduced in the mid-1960s, but home video recording would not take off until approximately a decade later. In 1975, Japanese electronics corporation Sony introduced the Betamax, the first home VCR. The Betamax offered one hour of recordable tape in a cassette. Soon after, Japan's Victor Company (JVC) came out with a similar machine that offered double that: two hours of recordable tape. Its product was called Video Home System (VHS). VHS quickly became the format of choice. As video sale and rental began increasing in popularity and more films became available in VHS-formatted tapes, Betamax sales declined, despite their reputation for sharper images and sound than the VHS.

In addition to playing films sold on videocassette tapes, VCRs could record television programs onto a blank videocassette tape. But Ramsay and Barton's device did more than a VCR. It would not only record any show the owner programmed it to record, but it could pause any live program being recorded as it was broadcast. After the viewer paused a live program for a few minutes, he or she could skip credits, any parts they thought were boring, and the commercials. This was a revolutionary concept.

BEYOND THE VCR

Before the invention of Ramsay and Barton's machine in 1997, the only way to skip television commercials was by prerecording a program on a VCR and fast-forwarding through the commercials during the playback. This could be inconvenient because the fast-forward and rewind functions displaying the sped-up image onscreen during playback were often only slightly faster than the program playing in real time. To get past the commercials more quickly, viewers had to stop the program completely and fast-forward while the program was not visible on the television screen. This meant they would often go too far and have to

Detail of a VCR's function buttons

rewind again, leading to a trial-and-error process: a loop of hitting play, stop, fast-forward/rewind, then play, stop, fast-forward/rewind again, and so on to reach a desired spot. With Ramsay and Barton's device, viewers could simply click a button and zoom past commercials in recorded shows. VCRs also could not pause live television while it was being recorded. Ramsay and Barton's DVR could.

After a few meetings and a consultation with a branding expert, Barton and Ramsay decided to

THE FIRST COMMERCIAL

The first television commercial aired in the United States on July 1, 1941. It was for Bulova watches. The slogan "America runs on Bulova time" ran below an image of a ticking clock placed over a map of the United States.[4] The commercial was aired at the start of a Philadelphia Phillies/Brooklyn Dodgers baseball game. Bulova paid just nine dollars, which would be approximately $130 today, for the commercial to air. Commercials today during popular events can cost millions of dollars to air.

change the name of the company in June 1998 from Teleworld to TiVo Inc., known as simply TiVo, which would also be the name of their product. The TiVo was unveiled for the first time at the annual Consumer Electronics Show in Las Vegas, Nevada, in January 1999. The TiVo created buzz leading up to its debut, and was anticipated as one of the hottest items at that year's show. The system was noticed both by show attendees, who got personal demonstrations of the system, and by journalists who reported on the device as "technology intended to change television forever."[3]

The TiVo developed a cultlike following soon after its introduction. Most consumers loved the idea of pausing live television and skipping commercials. Advertisers and powerful Hollywood television executives, however, were less than thrilled. Since the 1950s, the primary revenue source for television programs was the 30-second spot, a short commercial aired during and between television programs. The 30-second spot was an effective way to advertise products, events, and other television programs. Now Ramsay and Barton had invented a machine that could speed past these 30-second spots, and the hatred and fear in Hollywood was strong. Executives feared TiVo would destroy the $50 billion advertising industry. TiVo and its investors wondered how long it would take the television networks to succeed in shutting them down.

THE 30-SECOND SPOT

In the early days of television, advertisers embraced the idea that if consumers liked a particular television program, they would be more likely to buy a product associated with it. Many advertisers bought full sponsorship of a program, meaning they assumed most of the cost of production and had the right to use their name in the program's title. One example was Texaco Star Theater, a variety show featuring Milton Berle that aired in the late 1940s and early 1950s. Oil and natural gas company Texaco sponsored the show financially. Soap makers such as Palmolive and Ivory were common sponsors for daytime dramas, which is why these types of programs are known as soap operas.

In the early 1950s, television started becoming more sophisticated and more expensive to produce. It is estimated that from 1942 to 1952, costs associated with television production increased by 500 percent. Full sponsorship of programs became too expensive for most advertisers, and research showed that 30-second spots sold products just as effectively. By 1968, 80 percent of all television commercials had been reduced to 30 seconds in length.

In the late 1990s and early 2000s, analysts theorized that the TiVo, and similar DVR technology that followed, would drastically change the way consumers watched television and end commercial television as the public knew it. Whether the TiVo would bring about the downfall of commercial television remained to be seen. +

The TiVo created a lot of buzz in the technology world before,
during, and long after its initial unveiling.

Ramsay worked predominantly with computers during his early career.

THE FOUNDERS

TiVo founders Ramsay and Barton share an education and career background that led to many roles in the field of technology, sometimes within the same company. Their work on cutting-edge innovations prepared them for creating their own invention, which would one day alter the technology world.

MICHAEL RAMSAY

Michael Ramsay was born in Scotland in 1950. He grew up in Sighthill, a poor section of Edinburgh, Scotland, in the United Kingdom (UK). He received a bachelor of science degree, with high honors, in electrical engineering from Edinburgh University in 1972. At the beginning of his career, Ramsay was not interested in working with any aspect of television. He got his professional start in the 1970s working with a technology that was brand new at the time— desktop computers.

After graduating, Ramsay started work at an HP factory in Scotland. He visited the United States for the first time while working for HP in the mid-1970s.

HOMELAND HONORS

The Fellowship of Engineering was first established in 1976 and became the Royal Academy of Engineering in 1992. It is an institution in the United Kingdom that recognizes excellence in all fields of engineering through a variety of awards to professionals in the field.

Later in his career, Ramsay, a UK native, was awarded his homeland Academy's Sir Frank Whittle Medal in May 2006. Established to recognize creativity in engineering, the award is given to an "engineer, with strong connections with the United Kingdom, for outstanding and sustained achievement which has contributed to the well-being of the nation."[1]

At that time, the economy in the United Kingdom was awful—inflation was high, people were on strike, and it was not a great place to live or work. As fate would have it, Ramsay discovered he loved the United States. He decided to move to California in 1975.

SILICON VALLEY

Silicon Valley is the southern part of the San Francisco Bay Area of California, near Stanford University. Journalist Don Hoefler coined the name Silicon Valley in 1971 in a weekly newsletter describing the large number of electronic companies popping up in the Santa Clara County area of California. Silicon is a material used in semiconductors in computer circuits. Since the mid-1990s, Silicon Valley has been known as home to some of the world's most successful companies and has boasted the best-paying technology jobs in the country.

Ramsay and his wife settled in a region in the southern San Francisco Bay Area of California known as Silicon Valley, which is home to many technology companies. Within the valley is the HP headquarters, where Ramsay transferred. In 1980, Ramsay left HP for an opportunity at a new company, Convergent Technologies. The company's mission was developing a self-contained computer workstation. At the time, computers were the size of a whole room. The concept of a keyboard and a smaller central processing unit on an office desk was the cutting edge of technology. Computer companies were forming everywhere. Major companies such as International Business Machines (IBM) and Apple Inc. were just getting their start, and young engineers such as Microsoft founder Bill Gates and Apple founder Steve Jobs were inventing the future. It was an exciting time for Ramsay to be in the business.

In the late 1980s, Ramsay decided to return to an executive-level position at HP. In his new role, Ramsay hired Barton, among many others, to join his staff. However, it was not long before Ramsay realized he liked the atmosphere at a smaller company, such as Convergent Technologies, better than working for a big company, such as HP. Ramsay left HP for a second time when he was recruited by SGI, a special effects company with a staff of only a couple hundred people. Ramsay did well at SGI, rising to become senior vice president and general manager of the company's visual systems group. He was also involved in a division within SGI called Silicon Studio, creating interactive digital media applications. The special effects technology and the work environment at SGI excited Ramsay so much that he told Barton and some other friends about the opportunity. After hearing about it, Barton and the others all decided to leave HP at the same time and work for SGI. Working in the entertainment industry with products that filmmakers use to create

Barton first became interested in working with television during his time at SGI.

special effects was exciting, but going with a team of friends was likely even better.

JAMES BARTON

James Barton was born in 1958, right during the golden age of television, which played an important role in the Barton household when he was growing up. When Barton was a child, the television was often on. His favorite childhood show was *Star Trek*, and he watched so many episodes he could repeat a lot of the dialogue.

In 1980, Barton graduated from the University of Colorado at Boulder with a bachelor of science degree in electrical engineering. Two years later, in 1982, he also received a master of science degree in computer science at the University of Colorado at Boulder. Like his future business partner, Barton did not set out on a career path to work in television.

Barton started a career at technology company Bell Laboratories in Colorado while he was finishing his master's degree. He then took a job focusing on computers and computer networking at HP. But by the early 1990s, he found himself working on television and digital television projects at SGI. According to Ramsay, Barton's work at SGI included such inventions as one that made computer graphics applications work in real time. This was important because computer graphics needed to feel real and believable to a movie audience.

In 1995, Barton began working on a project with partner companies SGI and Time Warner Cable that aimed to add features to cable television. Coworker Ramsay was involved with the project as well. The project was a video-on-demand system called the Full-Service Network (FSN). It offered a test group of 4,000 households in Orlando, Florida, a system that delivered 500 channels of television programming and movies. In the mid-1990s, approximately 70 percent of television households subscribed to cable television, but the majority of them had access to only approximately 54 stations. The FSN system also allowed users to program their favorite shows, play interactive games, and shop at home. Users could even order pizza with just a click of the remote.

Unfortunately, another invention did exactly the same thing as the FSN at a lower cost: the Internet. The FSN system's technology was too expensive for consumers compared to the Internet. And people just seemed to prefer surfing the Internet from their home computers. The 18-month project never went further than 4,000 homes in Orlando.

Barton had been the lead system software architect for the FSN project. Although he loved working on the project, he did not like working with the large institutions in the television world such as cable and satellite companies. He felt as though they were monopolies and were moving backward.

Disillusioned by the failure of the FSN, Barton left SGI in 1996 to start his own company, Network Age Software. He hoped to apply what he had learned at SGI to the emerging technology of data management. At that time, movies played on the video-on-demand services were enormous files, many gigabytes of information. Barton wanted to create a way to manage and move large amounts of digital information. Barton may not have realized it when he quit SGI over the FSN failure, but sometimes the best ideas come out of the biggest failures.

A FATEFUL LUNCH

Over the years of working together at HP and SGI, Barton and Ramsay had formed

A FAILED PROJECT

The FSN that SGI and Time Warner Cable began in 1995 was a project more than two years in the making. Between preparation, hype, and delays, getting the system ready for the 4,000-home test group in Orlando was time consuming. At the time, it was the most ambitious experiment with interactive television to date, though other companies were rolling out similar programs.

The basic concept was that viewers could turn on their television and see a menu on the screen that gave options for selecting movies any time of day, shop in an electronic mall, and play realistic video games. It was anticipated that video-on-demand would be the most popular feature.

Unfortunately, with the investment in software production and fiber optics, the technology was expensive and the margin for a return on the investment was small. The point of the experiment in Orlando was to determine what features people would want, so executives would be prepared when expensive technology became more affordable in future years.

However, just as the FSN was being tested in Orlando in 1995, the World Wide Web was rapidly gaining users. The Internet promised the same service as the FSN, at a fraction of the cost.

a friendship. Ramsay left SGI for unclear reasons approximately a year after Barton. The two kept in touch after leaving SGI and met for lunch one afternoon in 1997. Over lunch, they kicked around some ideas and decided it might be fun to work together because they approached problem solving from different angles. Barton and Ramsay agreed they should start a company. Barton's company, Network Age Software, had been in start-up only approximately one year before he partnered with Ramsay. There had never been any real implementation of his new company's services when Barton instead decided to pursue a new venture with Ramsay.

After working on the FSN, Ramsay and Barton realized they loved the idea of developing something people could use in their homes. They thought their future company's new product should be something that would use digital technology—including manipulating music, television, or movies in their digital formats. The two continued meeting periodically to brainstorm their idea. Finally, it struck them that they could develop a home network server that would help people manage all three digital formats—television, movies, and music—and more. Barton and Ramsay's idea was to wire many different types of technology into a home computer server. The aim was to make life easier for the consumer by making it possible to control many devices from one place. In addition to movies, music, and television, the product would do things such as access voice mail, control the temperature in the house, and possibly even help with other household tasks such as turning on the vacuum cleaner or feeding the fish.

With this idea, Barton and Ramsay were ready to get their business going. Starting a business from the ground up can be quite difficult, however. It takes more than just a great idea. As Barton and Ramsay discovered, it takes hard work, a talented staff, a lot of money, and much personal risk to be successful. In fact, Barton's wife made him promise that no matter what he had to do for the company to be a success, he needed to make

TOO MANY APPS

Some additional ideas Ramsay and Barton considered including in the long list of home network apps: having a satellite connected to a home stereo allowing playback of music, downloading pictures from a camera to a computer, connecting the phone to a voice mail system, and controlling the timer on the coffee pot. The network would sync television, the refrigerator, the heating system, and more. No idea was off the table. "It was a field of dreams," said Barton.[2]

sure they did not lose their house. At the time, many Internet technology start-up companies were coming on the scene quickly and often failing just as fast, so this was a very real concern. +

Barton and Ramsay's partnership developed after they both quit work at SGI in the late 1990s.

Ramsay and Barton gave presentations all around
Silicon Valley in hopes of securing investors.

GETTING OFF THE GROUND

During many more brainstorming lunches, Barton and Ramsay developed their idea. Barton had more of an interest in the technological angle of the product, while Ramsay was more interested in managing people. It seemed like the perfect match for business leadership. In order to move forward, Barton and Ramsay had to pitch their idea to investors whom they hoped would fund the project.

CONVINCING INVESTORS

A challenge in starting any business is gathering the capital, or money, to get things off the ground. Many expenses are involved in starting and running a business: the property owner needs to be paid for the rental of the office space, supplies and materials must be purchased, and staff members require a paycheck. Someone needs to have the funds to pay these bills, which is where investors come in.

"If you don't do it you're going to wonder all your life should I have taken that shot or taken that chance. So go ahead and try."[1]

— *Jim Barton's advice on seeing ideas through*

Pitching an idea to investors is a lot like making an effective commercial. Business owners must be able to describe their new product idea to investors in simple terms. They need to be able to explain why the product is necessary in the marketplace and, more important, who is going to buy it. If the business owners are successful, an investor will buy into the business and give a large amount of money to get things started.

When investors buy into a company, they are taking a risk, making a bet that the company will succeed. In deciding to make that bet, investors want to know exactly how much money is required for startup and when the company will be profitable. In other words, the investors want to know when they will be getting the original money they loaned back and when they will begin making additional money on their investment. In 1997, Ramsay and Barton easily got appointments with venture capitalists all around Silicon Valley—they had

VENTURE CAPITALISM

Throughout US history, wealthy individuals and corporations have helped fund important construction projects such as canals and railroads as well as entire industries such as steel and automobiles. In the 1960s, a flood of wealthy business owners started becoming interested in new technology. They invested their own money in companies they felt had promise. Groups of investors would make deals to determine how much capital, or money, each would invest in a certain entrepreneur. They would create a partnership together and pool their money for a greater investment. Over time, these partnerships of investors evolved into venture capital firms. Venture capital firms regularly do business with entrepreneurs and independent investors interested in helping develop new companies in exchange for a chance in future profits. Venture capital is also sometimes called risk capital, as investors take a chance to get a business started.

a combined work history that made people very happy to meet with them. But Ramsay and Barton could not supply any of the needed investment predictions and product information in presentations to investors.

From the information they could give, Barton and Ramsay admitted to potential investors that it would be very expensive to develop their home server project. That alone scared many investors away. Ramsay and Barton also wanted to make customer service a top priority in their company, which is typically not the type of company investors like to fund. Investors prefer companies that promise to make money from the first day—not companies that need to develop consumer loyalty to be successful. Barton and Ramsay's first round of investor pitches in 1997 did not pan out as successfully as they had hoped. Only two investors were excited about the home server concept and had faith in the duo's abilities: Stewart Alsop of New Enterprise Associates (NEA) and Geoff Yang of Institutional Venture Partners (IVP).

Alsop and Yang both knew Barton and Ramsay from previous experiences at SGI. They knew the work ethic and knowledge the two founders brought to the table. They gave the company—then still known as Teleworld—a combined investment of $3 million for the home network server, mainly because they liked Barton and Ramsay's creative vision. Barton remembers Yang saying, "This is a crazy idea, I don't know how you're going to do it, but I'll bet you're going to come up with something."[2]

THE SHRINKING IDEA

Next, Barton and Ramsay had to figure out how to make their system work. The idea of the home server sounded great on paper, but unfortunately, it was not as good in practice. They spent a few months trying to figure out how to sync up, meaning connect and make work together, the needed technology. But the technology available in 1997 was both too expensive and too cumbersome to manage so many data forms—it simply had not caught up to their idea yet. In addition, Ramsay and Barton were having difficulty explaining their product in everyday terms. It had been easy to explain to other engineers around the drawing table what their system would do, but it was harder to explain to the general public. The public will not buy an idea if it does not understand why it needs it. That year, it became clear to the duo that the home network system was just not going to work. Their original concept had lasted only a couple of months.

With their idea fizzling, Barton and Ramsay were back to brainstorming. They realized that one component had been central to the home network server from the beginning: the ability to control television by manipulating digital data. "At the time, this server had a ton of apps that we thought up, one of which was DVR," said Ramsay. "We said, 'Look, you can't do everything. . . Let's decide on one app that we think is the killer app to run on it, and let's do that. If that's successful, then we'll branch out.'"[3]

As journalist Michael Lewis of the *New York Times* explained Barton and Ramsay's simplified idea, "Instead of transforming the entire American home, they decided to focus on the one

"TiVo's courtship of investors over the next couple of years was impressive. By venture capital standards, it wasn't exactly a big draw. The company had an expensive business model, was creating a new consumer electronics category, was subsidizing hardware, was service- and subscription-oriented, and wouldn't be profitable for years. But Ramsay and Barton's vision for customized television proved too strong to resist."[4]

— *Christine Y. Chen,*
Fortune *magazine*

appliance that was the closest thing to the center of attention in the American home: the television."[5] Barton remembers sitting around brainstorming one afternoon when someone asked, "Wouldn't it be great if you could pause live television?"[6] The idea sparked. The team went back to the original investors in early 1998 and explained they had a new idea— one that would be simpler and easier to explain to the consumer. ☩

"We went back to the VCs [venture capitalists] and said, "Thank you very much for the money. We've changed our minds. Here's what we're going to do instead and here's why we think it's a good idea." They said, 'Oh, that sounds just like a VCR.' So we had this challenge of explaining [that it was not]."[7]

—*Mike Ramsay on presenting the new idea to investors*

With the revolutionary idea to pause live television, Ramsay and Barton's futures—and the future of television—were about to change.

Ramsay and Barton created machines with a sleek, simple design.

CREATING TIVO

Where the home server network idea flopped, the focused vision of manipulating television succeeded. The original investors loved Ramsay and Barton's new idea and approved moving forward with the change.

The new product would be a simple black box that connected to consumers' televisions. Future systems would be embedded as part of cable boxes, but the first unit was a stand-alone device. Using a hard disk, the software allowed users to record up to 14 hours of programming and play back any recorded television program they wanted using a remote control. As an extension of the television, the device would be intuitive to use, with no power switch or reset button. Said Ramsay,

> When we started . . . we wrote a list of core principles for our company to follow. One of them was "It just works," meaning everything has to work in the most fundamental, easy, intuitive way possible. The principles were strong from day one and set the tone for how our products were created and how we treated our employees.[1]

Barton knew from his experience with the FSN that he could build a system that was both simple to use and did what it promised: record, play back, and pause live television.

BUILDING A STAFF

According to Ramsay, one of the most important aspects in starting a business is finding the best and brightest core staff. Ramsay and Barton knew they had a good leadership team, but they needed to find a team of engineers and support staff that could help them realize their vision. Ramsay and Barton both wanted to produce something that was easy to use and affordable for the consumer. They also wanted to build a creative work environment that would attract the type of talented individuals who would be excited about their product. Once they had this group in place, they felt their company and idea would move forward fast.

As the partner responsible for the day-to-day operation of the company, Ramsay took on the task of hiring. When interviewing potential employees, Ramsay placed more value on his personal connection to someone than on the candidate's expertise in a certain area. Ramsay hired people he liked, not people who had ever necessarily done the job before. After all, no one on the initial management team had ever done his or her particular job before—it was new to everyone. They hired a team of engineers who were interested in the idea of producing a complex machine that looked simple on the outside.

By the end of 1997, Teleworld had a staff of 12 and an office. But the company name had only been temporary when it was chosen; Barton and Ramsay had known all along they would eventually rename the company. With a new product direction, it came time for a new name. Ramsay hired designer Michael Cronan to come up with some suggestions for names and to help develop a brand that would identify their product. The staff helped to narrow down 800 possible new company names by simply picking the names they liked best. Cronan recalls that from the whittled-down list of approximately 100 strong contenders, TiVo was the ninth name he presented to the team.

Cronan liked the concept of a television evolution, or "TiVolution"—TiVo for short.[2] The name TiVo also reminded him of the rock band Devo, whose members had a philosophy of de-evolution, or backward evolution, which was going back

CREATING A BRAND

Branding is an important part of any business plan. The brand is what people see and associate with a product. A company's brand is created through things such as the name, logo, and the company Web site. Famous brands are able to communicate an entire message in a symbol, such as the golden arches that symbolize McDonald's.

"Once we settled on the name, we began work on creating the identity. I wanted to provide a kind of identity that would become as recognizable as the mouse ears are to Disney," said Cronan. "From that impulse I placed a smile under the word that would make a face out of the lettering and signal the happy attitude of the character. . . . I was driving one day and saw the little Darwinian fish-with-legs evolution character on a bumper and immediately realized that TiVo needed legs."[3]

The character in the TiVo logo is called the TiVo Guy.

and making something right from its primitive state. The name TiVo stuck, capitalizing on the idea that they were beginning a television evolution that would change the very basics of how programs were watched.

DEVELOPMENT

With a brand name established, the TiVo team was ready to start development. Barton took on the primary responsibility for product design and initial development.

Technical challenges are involved in developing any product, and the TiVo was no exception. Creating a prototype, or test model, helped work out some of the glitches. Once they had working models of the prototype, the TiVo leadership team gave units to its stockholders, including Yang and Alsop, and staff members to use at home. A number of problems were identified this way and fixed before the machine was unveiled. Thanks to a talented and enthusiastic group of engineers, the first working prototype for the TiVo DVR was ready for exhibition.

THE UNVEILING

The TiVo was revealed at the 1999 Consumer Electronics Show in Las Vegas. It is the largest annual consumer technology trade show in the world. Technology innovations such as the compact disc (CD), Microsoft Xbox, plasma TV, camcorder, and more have been unveiled there each January since 1967. Even before the 1999 show, consumers and the media were excited about the TiVo. Journalists wrote about it as something that would change the world—or at least the world of television. The buzz the unveiling created was a promising kickoff. However, it also created huge pressure for Ramsay and Barton's little company.

After introducing the TiVo to the media and public, Barton and Ramsay knew they needed to make it available very quickly or risk losing the momentum and interest that had been created. It was time to produce the actual units to sell.

THE BLUE MOON CHALLENGE

To develop a product ready for the marketplace would realistically require at least four months of work. However, Ramsay issued a challenge to the staff. He wanted them to produce and ship a working DVR by the end of March 1999—less than three months after the electronics show. After gasps and complaints about how impossible it would be to turn the prototype into a polished system ready for production in such a short period of time, the staff got to work. Ramsay contracted with consumer electronics company Philips to produce the boxes that would run the software. In the office, the TiVo staff called the challenge "the Blue Moon project"—a code name that referred to the second full moon that would occur at the end of March that year.[4] People ate and slept at their desks—in fact, one of the office hall closets held spare blankets and pillows—working around the clock to meet the tight deadline. Said Barton,

> *We had to figure out how to make this thing work reliably and work all the time, like a television. It has to work when your power goes out and work when your power comes back on, and the only way we're going to get there is by not putting any crutches on the product. We had to force ourselves to get it right.*[5]

In the end, the hard work paid off. On the last day of March, the first TiVo machines rolled off the production line and were shipped. Ramsay declared that from then on, March 31 would be known as the "Blue Moon" holiday for TiVo employees.[6]

STAFF FIELD TRIPS

To celebrate the successful completion of the Blue Moon challenge in March 1999, the whole staff took a field trip to the third-party manufacturing plant in Milpitas, California, where the TiVo DVRs were being made. The staff wore blue jackets and caps and watched the units come off the manufacturing line. Later in the year, the same group went to a number of retail stores in the San Francisco Bay Area to give demos and help customers get more information about the TiVo.

PATENTS

The TiVo basically plugs into a television and records like a VCR, but with more advanced features and capabilities. One of the most important features of the TiVo is its ability to record and play back, pause, and then fast-forward and rewind, all at the same time. This feature, called Time Warp, was so key to the TiVo's unique success that the company had filed for a patent in 1998, prior to unveiling its first model. "Figuring that one out was critical, and had not really been done before—simultaneously recording and playing back video in a very low-cost way that 'just worked,'" said Ramsay.[7] Although a complex machine was inside, they wanted TiVo to be interpreted as an easy-to-use machine. Barton and Ramsay knew they needed positive word of mouth reinforcing this feature to get their product off the ground. As long as TiVo users could simply hit a button and get what they wanted, it seemed their product would be a success. Time Warp was just one of many patents TiVo would file—and need to legally defend—in future years.

Another technical challenge, and patent filed for, concerned programming information. TiVo engineers had to figure out how the machine's digital program guide would work. The TiVo had to provide users with a correct listing of available shows and the times they aired. If a user wanted to record *Grey's Anatomy*, for instance, the data about the channel and time the show aired would have to be accurate or the machine might end up recording *CSI* instead.

At the time, the usual way for companies to gather data about television programming was to call local television stations and manually write down their program schedules. Taking into account the many cable services and channels, TiVo had to coordinate with close to 65,000 different combinations in order for users in every region of the United States to have an accurate program guide available on their TiVo. During TiVo's first year, it filed for a

EARLY TV GUIDES

The first two licensed commercial television stations went on the air in New York on July 1, 1941. The first printed television program guide was issued the day before, on June 30.

Because these stations broadcast for only a few hours each day, the program guides were very short. The guides were printed in newspapers or mailed directly to customers. At that time, there were only 7,000 television sets in the entire country.

As television channels and programming multiplied, the program guides became longer and more complicated to compile. In 1953, three regional print magazines—New York's *Television Guide*, Chicago's *Television Forecast*, and Philadelphia's *TV Digest*—were combined to create a new national magazine called *TV Guide*. *TV Guide* was printed weekly and made available by subscription, which stands today.

patent for its Program Guide, which would be able to provide accurate data in all available service areas for its customers. In order to do this, the units needed a modem installed so the DVR could access television data over the telephone line.

The unit also needed to be secure to prevent people from hacking into it to steal their neighbor's programs or see what their neighbors were watching. The TiVo team also wanted to prevent the device from receiving data that could break it. To ensure the security of the system, the team created a service called Phone Home. If anything went wrong internally in an individual unit, the machine would go into safe mode and shut down. The Phone Home service would communicate through the modem to the home server and reboot the machine. Most users would never know there had been a problem. And that was the way the TiVo team liked it. +

HACKING

Computer hackers are computer enthusiasts with a great deal of talent and knowledge about computers. They intentionally hack into computer systems for control or information. Hackers can often get computers to override programs and security systems, and they sometimes break into computer systems as a practical joke or because they think it is fun. Others may break into computers to steal information that can be used in a harmful way against the owner. The TiVo is just one technological device that must protect itself against hackers. Computers and other software often use preventative programs and internal security systems to protect users' information.

TiVo applications were quite complex, effectively managing
large amounts of program data.

Despite the buzz surrounding its rollout, the TiVo did not sell very well in the beginning, likely due to steep prices.

CONVINCING THE PUBLIC

I t did not take long after the initial rollout for consumers to discover TiVo, but the company did not grow as fast as Ramsay and Barton had imagined or hoped. Although many thought the concept behind the TiVo was new and exciting, the company had to overcome many hurdles to gain initial widespread acceptance by both consumers and entertainment executives.

BUYING AND USING THE TIVO

It surprised the TiVo team that consumers did not embrace the system more quickly, especially since all of the staff had tried the units at home and now could not imagine watching television without it. One of the barriers for the public could have been the relatively high price. When the units first went on sale at retail stores in 1999, they sold for approximately $500. Once the TiVo was plugged into a wall outlet and connected to the television and cable or satellite service, for users with cable or satellite, it was ready to record.

Originally, the box also had a modem installed inside that connected to a phone line. Once the modem was connected, the TiVo dialed into the main server at TiVo headquarters and downloaded the specific program guide for the zip code where it was located to its hard drive. Newer models work much the same way—the TiVo is plugged into the wall and connected to the television. The only difference is updates are received by connecting to the Internet through a wired or wireless connection rather than telephone dial-up. For users without Internet connections, however, the TiVo can still connect through a phone line with an adapter.

To access a connection, a service subscription fee of approximately ten dollars per month was also required on top of the device price for the program guide service. The fee covered the program guide, but also a secure server designed to never break down.

"Television has a bad rep, it's kind of broken. When you have 500 channels and there's nothing on, television is definitely broken. I think what TiVo has done is put people back in charge. And that's a primal, important thing that people like as far as a social trend that's far broader than television . . . they get very excited and love it. . . . That's a huge motivator for us as a company."[1]

— *Mike Ramsay on the motivation behind TiVo*

Users also had the option of paying an up-front fee of a few hundred dollars to receive a lifetime subscription to the guide service, which was good for the life of the TiVo unit. The lifetime subscription would intermittently be revoked and reinstated by TiVo in coming years due to low monthly revenues, but was reinstated indefinitely as of 2012. Although the concept stirred interest, many people did not have a reason to believe they

Ramsay and Barton continue to promote TiVo
to the media and consumers.

really needed a TiVo, making both the unit price and
service fee major deterrents.

COURTING CUSTOMERS AND THE PRESS

The TiVo team had to convince consumers they
needed a TiVo. Ramsay and Barton addressed this
challenge as they branded TiVo. Their philosophy
for the company was "TV My Way."[2] The TiVo

Season Pass™

Choose your favorite shows and the TiVo service will automatically record every episode, whenever it airs.

WishList™

Got a favorite actor? Special hobby? The TiVo service will find and record programs based on your interests.

Features Season Pass and Wish List were immediate favorites among consumers.

would give consumers the power to watch the television programs they wanted when they wanted. The marketing centered on how easy the TiVo was to use and on the fact that consumers would be in control of their television viewing for the first time in history.

To show people the benefits of the product, the entire staff split into groups and set up live demonstrations in local retail stores after the first units shipped at the end of March. Showing people how the system worked and letting them use the remote to pause live television being recorded created a buzz of excitement. People particularly loved a feature called Season Pass that could be programmed to record an entire season of a show. They also loved a feature called Wish List, which could be used to find and automatically record any program featuring a particular actor, director, or keyword.

Once the public was interested, Ramsay and Barton stopped spending money on expensive advertising. Word of mouth seemed to be more effective as enthusiastic TiVo users started writing articles and spreading the word.

As TiVo was wooing customers, it was getting mixed reviews in the press. Members of the press who were more consumer-orientated loved the TiVo because it was simple and easy to use. Those who were more interested in the technical aspects disliked it because they thought it was not technologically impressive enough.

PUBLIC REACTIONS

Television executives initially hated the idea of TiVo. By allowing viewers to skip commercials, TiVo was essentially promising viewers access to entertainment without "paying" advertisers or networks.[3] Eventually, however, most of the major networks changed their opinions. Numerous cable and satellite companies made investments or partnered with TiVo. By investing in the company, they at least had some say in how the technology developed.

Users warmed up to TiVo more quickly, as did some members of the media. Consumers and product reviewers praised TiVo: "It's changed my life, I can never go back!"[4] "I'm wondering how I lived without it! I'm not watching more TV, just better TV."[5] Some members of the media were only slightly more reserved.

Journalist Michael Lewis equated the founding date of TiVo with the birth of successful Internet commerce company Amazon.com and Internet consumer-to-consumer corporation eBay along the time line of important dates in technology development. Not all members of the media had praise for TiVo, however. Some thought the TiVo was too complicated for the average television viewer and the company would soon fizzle out.

APPEASING ADVERTISERS AND NETWORKS

Network executives were panicking about how the TiVo would change the way viewers watched television and commercials. Barton and Ramsay knew networks that relied on advertising to make their money were going to be afraid of, if not downright hostile about, their device. During its initial rollout, TiVo had to walk a thin line between advertising something consumers thought was great—skip the commercials!—while downplaying that same fact to the television industry.

Barton and Ramsay addressed the fears of television networks and advertisers honestly and directly. They made presentations to network executives, likely as a preemptive move to explain their product and avoid lawsuits that could put TiVo out of business. They wanted to try to address any concerns before they became too big. The networks' biggest fear was the loss of commercials—a concern that caused one executive to ask Ramsay if he was "the devil" during a presentation he gave to television executives in 1999.[6] Popular shows at the time, such as *Survivor* and *American Idol*, sold their advertising space for millions of dollars per minute.

To address concerns, TiVo met its opponents halfway. Ramsay and Barton downplayed the aspect of skipping commercials in presentations. They pointed

"I was more than happy to build a device that could allow you to skip over [commercials]. At the same time, we knew that the networks especially who derived all their revenue from advertising would be very nervous about this technology. So we went to them very early on at TiVo we said 'look at what we're building,' we said, 'this thing's coming. . .' but in years down the road it's going to be very common and what you should do, is get on board now. In fact, we think you should invest in TiVo. And make sure that instead of running away from this thing, that you're part of it."[7]

—*Jim Barton*

out that their system had been designed so viewers could fast-forward through commercials, but not skip them altogether, so product advertisement was not entirely lost. This placated the networks in that the commercial would still make an impression on the viewer, even though it might be in a blurry, high-speed way.

During the presentations, Ramsay and Barton also worked hard to communicate ideas for alternative sources of revenue other than commercials. They assured television executives they could provide something better than the traditional commercial. They promised the ability to program messages to pop up into recorded programs that would advertise next week's show or another show on a program recorded earlier. Viewers could also hit a button and find out more about a particular product being advertised if they were interested. This would help networks and ad executives target

TIVO TAGS

TiVo's ideas for alternatives to commercials came to fruition in 2002, when it started selling something called tags. Viewers would see an icon appear over commercials even as they fast-forwarded past them. They could click on the tag with their remote to enter a contest, get a free DVD, or watch a longer commercial. The first tags were for car company Lexus and Best Buy. Eventually, General Motors, Nissan Motors, Coca-Cola, Walt Disney World, and Royal Caribbean cruise line all paid for TiVo tags.

their products more specifically to the consumers they were trying to reach.

TiVo had another plan to appease the executives. With the Phone Home modem, TiVo had more intimate access to consumers' viewing information than the networks did. By collecting data from their customers through the modem, TiVo could report to the networks exactly what people watched and what programs they recorded. TiVo promised the television executives and advertisers that it could deliver patterns of viewing—what the viewer was watching minutes before and what they watched immediately after a certain program. And, most important to the networks, TiVo could report on which commercials its customers chose to watch or skip over.

PRIVACY CONCERNS

With the plan to garner information on the programs its users watched, TiVo was in a place to charge a fee to anyone wanting that gathered information about the viewing demographic. Unfortunately, though this strategy had soothed the nerves of executives in Hollywood, it brought up serious issues of breach of privacy for consumers. Barton himself was concerned about issues of privacy and had made sure the system he constructed could not save or share personal data about the customer's identity. It would just share information about which shows they recorded, and watch for trends in their viewing. The company hoped these tactics would both satisfy the television industry and avoid lawsuits.

This created another complexity to TiVo's plan, however. In order to gather this valuable information, TiVo had to get into as many American households as possible. To deliver on the promises made to the networks and advertising executives, it needed buy-ins from bigger investors in order to produce and sell many, many more units. At the same time, rival companies were also producing DVRs, creating intense competition. Ramsay and Barton realized they had to find partners. +

TiVo needed to get into many households so it could gather viewing information for the networks.

Main Menu

Channel Guide
Replay Guide
Photo Viewer
Find Shows
Manual Record
Replay Zones
View Shows by Category
Messages
Setup

replaytv
There's always something good on.

ReplayTV was initially more expensive than TiVo,
but it did not charge a subscription fee.

COMPETITORS, PARTNERS, AND AN IPO

Although Ramsay and Barton's idea was revolutionary, it was not theirs alone. From the beginning, they faced competition. However, competition can drive survival. To secure and maintain the top spot in the DVR market, TiVo had to be better than competitors' versions right out of the gate. It also had to continue being the best.

COMPETITOR: REPLAYTV

ReplayTV had unveiled a similar DVR at the same time as TiVo—at the Las Vegas Consumer Electronics Show in January 1999. The press exploited the competition during that first year and often asked about it during interviews. Ramsay was even asked to pose on a magazine cover with the CEO of ReplayTV, Anthony Wood, in a pretend duel with remote controls. Some of the staff were upset by the intense competition, but victory was sweet for TiVo.

ReplayTV was received more negatively by the television networks than TiVo. Its units allowed viewers to completely skip commercials—not just fast-forward

SONICBLUE BUYS REPLAYTV

Former electronics company SonicBlue purchased ReplayTV in 2001 for $120 million. The company remained more controversial than TiVo to the television networks, as it continued producing boxes designed to completely skip commercials. In addition, SonicBlue incorporated a feature that allowed users to share the content they recorded with friends. This practice caused the company numerous lawsuits.

past them, as with the TiVo. Some journalists felt TiVo had missed the boat in not offering users the same feature, but TiVo claimed its competitor's ability to skip over commercials completely was equal to piracy. With the TiVo, viewers would still see snippets of the commercials, albeit at a faster speed. As a result of its more renegade technology, ReplayTV was sued multiple times by the television industry. Relative to the life of the company, the competition didn't last long. ReplayTV altered its model and licensed the technology. In 2001, SonicBlue bought out ReplayTV. The company filed for bankruptcy two years later over many lawsuits related to the technology.

PARTNERS: DIRECTV AND AOL

TiVo organized partnerships to keep the excitement going about its product. A deal with satellite company DIRECTV looked particularly lucrative in 1999. That April, DIRECTV agreed to supply its customers with the TiVo DVR as part of its service package.

TiVo was also able to attract the interest of Internet and media company America Online (AOL) with the help of investor and philanthropist

With millions of subscribers, satellite provider DIRECTV
gave TiVo valuable exposure.

Paul Allen, who had cofounded giant software
corporation Microsoft with Bill Gates. In 2000, AOL
invested $200,000 and signed a three-year contract
with TiVo to include its DVR technology as part of
its interactive television that was in development,
called AOLTV. AOLTV would combine Internet
access, e-mail, instant messaging, and TiVo DVR
technology in one unit that would be made by
electronics company Philips.

MICROSOFT COFOUNDER PAUL ALLEN

In 1975, Paul Allen cofounded Microsoft with Bill Gates. After leaving Microsoft in 1983, he founded Vulcan Inc. as a way to invest in projects that change the way people live and work through "arts, education, entertainment, sports, business, and technology."[1] Throughout his career, he has invested more than $1 billion, making him one of America's top philanthropists.

COMPETITORS: MICROSOFT . . . AND DIRECTV

Around the same time DIRECTV partnered with TiVo, it also made a big surprise decision that had TiVo scrambling. DIRECTV made a deal with Microsoft to offer customers an alternative to the TiVo, likely for financial gain. The Microsoft version of the DVR would be offered along with DIRECTV satellite services, similar to the arrangement the company made with TiVo. DIRECTV planned on marketing both products equally to its customers.

Established software company Microsoft had been around since 1976, which meant it had more resources and many more years of experience than TiVo. Ramsay and Barton were understandably worried about the competition. In the end, however, people preferred

The Sony headquarters in Tokyo, Japan

the TiVo to the Microsoft product. Even though DIRECTV did indeed market each product fairly to its customers, Microsoft soon gave up.

PARTNER: SONY

Because of their expertise with electronics, companies that manufactured DVD players and VCRs became natural competitors for TiVo. After the scare with Microsoft, the TiVo founders were worried about other consumer electronics companies swooping in to compete in the DVR market. Working with potential competitors, rather than against them, helped TiVo get several licensing deals. Licensing technology is an agreement where the technology owner allows another company to use, modify, and even resell the technology in exchange for compensation. Rather than waiting around for the eventual competition, TiVo approached electronics company Sony, offering to license its technology to the company for a fee. TiVo established a partnership with Sony in September 1999. Sony made a deal to purchase 2.6 million shares of TiVo stock at the negotiated lower rate of $10.41 per share, for a total investment of more than $27.5 million. As a part of the partnership, Sony also secured a seat on the TiVo board—giving Sony a say in decision making. Some journalists criticized TiVo for the if-you-can't-beat-'em-join-'em attitude it had developed.

INITIAL PUBLIC OFFERING

By the end of September 1999, TiVo had sold 18,000 units. Now that it had established itself as a promising company, TiVo was ready to sell its stock to the public in an initial public offering (IPO).

People can buy stocks to invest in a company they think will be profitable. The more a company is worth, the higher its stock price is. Stock prices for TiVo started at $16 per share, but so many people were buying the stock that by the end of the day, the price had gone up to $78. In a very short time, the company's value had skyrocketed into the billions of dollars. Ramsay thought they had "died and gone to heaven."[2]

By the end of 1999, the TiVo had taken on a life of its own, garnering many favorable reviews and positive customer feedback. Ramsay was initially very happy with sales considering the TiVo was a scaled back version of a

IPO BASICS

Companies typically have an IPO to generate excitement and funding. As Canadian consulting firm Deloitte explains,

Going public signifies, to both the company's executives and the outside world, that the company has achieved a special kind of success. Overnight, the company will be transformed from a closely held entity with a handful of shareholders to a company with a large number of holders of stock that can be easily bought or sold.[3]

Anybody who buys stock technically owns a small portion of that company. If a company's profits go up, the stocks are worth more, and if the company's profits go down, the stocks are worth less. Prices of stocks can fluctuate daily. Although having an IPO is largely seen as a positive thing, it does carry some disadvantages. A partial list from Deloitte includes less control by the company, a required disclosure of company information, and pressure on the company to continue growing.

bigger idea. He thought that after the company sold a few thousand TiVo units, it would go back to the "real thing"— the original home network idea.[4] But, as the TiVo took off, he realized this *was* the real thing. +

TiVo started trading on the US stock market, headquartered in the
NASDAQ building in New York City.

The Federal Trade Commission Building in Washington DC

SURVIVING

By 2001, competitors' products were fizzling, licensing deals TiVo offered had hopefully appeased other potential competitors, and partnerships with heavyweight electronics companies were secured. It appeared TiVo would continue on an upswing in its first few years.

Unfortunately, despite TiVo's safeguards to avoid lawsuits when selling viewer demographic information, the federal government became involved in 2001.

PRIVACY INVESTIGATION

In March of that year, Congressman Edward Markey, a member of the Subcommittee on Telecommunications and the Internet, questioned TiVo's information-gathering practices after receiving a letter from a TiVo customer who was concerned about all the data going back and forth over his modem. Markey wrote to the Federal Trade Commission (FTC), an organization that ensures business practices are fair to both consumers and competitors. He requested that the FTC investigate TiVo on its collection and use of customer information.

In May, Robert Pitofsky of the FTC stated in a letter to Congressman Markey that TiVo's practices of customer information collection did not warrant any action by the FTC. Based on the FTC's investigation, it found:

THE INTERNET BUBBLE

The Internet bubble of the late 1990s made household names of companies such as Yahoo, Google, and Amazon.com. It also created many forgettable companies that crashed and burned right out of the gate. Some start-up companies made millions for their investors when their stocks ballooned in price overnight. Between November 1999 and March 2000, more than 200 Internet companies offered IPOs, flooding the market. Most of these companies never saw a profit, but were selling stock shares at a high rate. By December 2000, the total value of the more than 370 Internet companies in existence had fallen by 75 percent. More than $1 trillion of combined value vanished. When these companies failed, investors lost a lot of money.

TiVo did in fact collect personally identifiable TV viewing information, but only from customers from whom it first obtained consent.; for the vast majority of customers, the TV viewing information was transmitted from the TiVo Receiver and collected and stored by TiVo, in an anonymous manner.[1]

The report then elaborated that TiVo collected two types of information from a user's TiVo receiver: viewing information and personal data on the TiVo receiver's operation and serial number, but that these two types of information "are kept separate during the transmission and stored in separate locations."[2]

THE BUBBLE BURSTS

In addition to the scare from the FTC investigation, 2001 was not

A failed dot-com company prepares to auction its technology in 2001;
a common scene during the bubble burst that year.

a good time to be a start-up company. Too many
Internet start-up companies had flooded the market
during the late 1990s and then quickly failed. This
time came to be known as the Internet bubble burst,
or dot-com bubble burst. In its wake, investors were
wary of investing in new companies and held onto
the money they had left.

Although TiVo survived the infamous dot-com
bubble burst, it did not come out unscathed. The
company made some difficult decisions in order to
stay in business. One of the hardest was in 2001
when Ramsay and Barton laid off a number of their

staff, whom they had come to think of as family. The layoffs came after several of the licensing deals TiVo had made fell through mere months after the deals were signed, causing TiVo's funds to dwindle to just a few million dollars in the bank. Then successful electronics company Best Buy approached TiVo in 2002. The company had stores across the nation and was interested in partnering with TiVo as distributors of the TiVo Series2, released December 2001, which had 60 hours of recording time. The TiVo team breathed a collective sigh of relief.

NEW RESPECT FOR TIVO

In another positive turn of events, TiVo's more moderate stance on commercials as compared to its competitor ReplayTV ended up creating good will among entertainment executives. Entertainment companies that had initially been against TiVo ended up respecting the company's business practices.

ReplayTV had not only targeted and eliminated commercials for users, but it lost even more respect by allowing users to share programs over the Internet. "That crossed the line," Ramsay said. "They got sued. They were the bad guy; therefore, we were the good guy."[3] TiVo not only won the respect of companies that had initially rallied against them, but some of those companies invested in TiVo as well. A group of companies—including Disney, Viacom, Discovery Communications, NBC, Showtime, HBO, and Time Warner—invested approximately $50 million in TiVo. These investments made the difference for TiVo's survival in the wake of the Internet bubble burst.

LEADERSHIP CHANGES

By January 2003, TiVo had survived and was thriving. In May, Ramsay and Barton hired Marty Yudkovitz, an executive who had served as vice president at NBC, to serve as the new president of the company and help establish brand recognition. Ramsay, who had been serving as the president, now

CEO, PRESIDENT, CTO, COO

Most companies have a complex organizational chart with positions including president and chief executive officer (CEO). Many also have a board of directors who offer advice and help make important decisions.

In general, the CEO is the highest-ranking executive in a company, with the president being second in command. Some companies also have parallel positions, such as the chief technology officer (CTO) and the chief operating officer (COO). Generally speaking, the CTO is in charge of the research and development of products and technology needs for the company. The COO is usually in charge of the day-to-day running of the company. Both report to the CEO. Some companies have no president, but have senior vice president–level positions that are equal to the CTO and COO ranking. A whole committee is often involved in making important decisions.

took on the dual roles of board chair and chief operating officer (COO). Barton kept his title of chief technology officer (CTO).

Nearing the end of 2003, things were in a better place, and TiVo's next hope was that the company would finally start making a profit. The company was approaching a critical measurement—the sale of its one-millionth DVR. TiVo was not slowing down as it approached this milestone. It pushed toward new licensing partnerships, continued providing networks with advertising opportunities and demographic data, and brainstormed new and exciting services to give its customers.

In November 2003, TiVo sold its one-millionth unit. But profits did not follow as quickly as the company had hoped. In light of this, both Barton and Ramsay started thinking about more changes to the leadership of the company. +

Yudkovitz became president of TiVo in 2003,
but his stint would be brief.

EchoStar Communications' DVR, installed with Dish Network satellite service, had applications that incited a lawsuit from TiVo.

DARK DAYS

In January 2004, TiVo had more than profits to worry about. Multinational technology company EchoStar Communications, the parent company of cable provider Dish Network, was offering satellite service boxes that came with DVR capabilities. TiVo claimed the EchoStar Communications DVR had capabilities that infringed on its Time Warp patent, issued to TiVo in 2001. Defending its patent, TiVo filed a lawsuit against EchoStar that year. It would be seven years before the litigation for the complicated suit would come to conclusion.

ANOTHER DIRECTV SURPRISE

TiVo's ongoing financial struggle only worsened after taking legal action against EchoStar. While TiVo had been striving for years to make a profit, the complete opposite happened in 2005. DIRECTV, one of TiVo's first partners, and through whom two-thirds of TiVo boxes had been sold, gave TiVo its second surprise in two years. In January, DIRECTV announced it would be building its own DVR technology into its units. Losing one of its oldest partnerships did not bode well for TiVo. TiVo lost $79.8 million that year when its stock fell to under four dollars a share. To recover from the damage created by the DIRECTV situation, Ramsay announced a new business strategy in early 2005: TiVo would go back to selling its units independent of a cable or satellite company.

Ramsay stepped down as TiVo CEO in 2005, but he would remain involved in the company he cofounded.

RAMSAY STEPS DOWN AS CEO

Later that month, Ramsay made another big announcement. He planned to step down as the CEO as soon as a replacement could be hired. Ramsay felt he could more effectively maintain the vision of forward motion of the company in a different role. He would stay on as the chairman of the board.

Just after Ramsay's announcement, TiVo President Yudkovitz announced his imminent departure from the company. Yudkovitz claimed his reason for leaving was to spend more time with his family, but journalists speculated he had never been the right fit to move the company forward as president.

Many analysts, including some members of the TiVo board, felt these changes would be good for the company. Even though Ramsay had been the leader who rallied the team, as an engineer he had never been willing to give up certain controls. He had maintained a high level of brand control when it came to making deals with cable companies, which some analysts felt had cost TiVo lucrative partnerships. With Ramsay in a different role, someone else might be more open to compromising with companies that were potential partners, giving TiVo new life, even if it meant less control over the use of its product.

Since 2003, Tom Rogers—a high-level executive who had worked on the US House of Representative's telecommunications committee as well as at NBC— had been on the TiVo board. In the fall of 2004, he was appointed the vice chairman of the TiVo board. In 2005, Rogers brokered a new deal with Comcast,

TOM ROGERS

Tom Rogers, CEO of TiVo, is confident about where the company is headed. He says, "Our future seems to be very much about being able to provide answers to operators."[1] Always ready for a challenge, he enjoys being able to provide solutions to TiVo partners, retailers, and users. For some partners, TiVo software is installed in a DVR box manufactured by another company. As an alternative, TiVo can install the software as an additional option to an existing service—essentially giving customers two DVR services in one unit. Rogers loves the "flexibility in terms of [TiVo's] future as to how we actually get the TiVo experience in front of users."[2]

a cable company based out of Philadelphia. It was TiVo's first major deal with a cable company. Just as DIRECTV had done with satellite service customers, Comcast would sell the TiVo DVR services to its cable service customers. TiVo shares rose by $2.87, or 75 percent, to $6.70 on March 15, 2005, the day the deal with Comcast was announced. A few months later, on July 1, Rogers became the new CEO of TiVo. Rogers hit the ground running by assuring the TiVo founders that his primary goal was increasing the number of subscribers by enhancing relationships with partners and examining the marketing strategy.

The TiVo remained a top DVR choice as of 2005. That year, approximately 6.5 million people owned DVRs and almost a third of them were TiVo customers. However, the 6.5 million people that owned DVRs was less than

5 percent of the 109 million television households in 2005. Although it was making sales, TiVo had hoped to make a profit by 2003, five years after founders Ramsay and Barton started the company—but this goal still eluded TiVo in 2005.

In the spring of 2006, the TiVo Series2 DT 80 and 180 were released. The *DT* stood for "dual tuner"; two shows could be recorded at once. The two versions available offered either 80 or 180 hours of recording time. Another updated TiVo was revealed later that fall: the TiVo Series3 could record approximately 30 hours of high definition (HD) programming or up to approximately 300 hours of standard definition (SD) programming. HD television takes up more memory but has higher contrast and resolution and better accuracy and saturation of color. Some Series3 features were not fully equipped for HD, however. The price was also high, nearing $800. In 2007, the company introduced the TiVo HD, which left out price-hiking

TIVO'S EMMY AWARD

In 2006, the Academy of Television Arts & Sciences awarded TiVo an Emmy Award for outstanding achievement in enhanced television programming. The Interactive Television Emmy Awards recognized TiVo for "original interactive television programming content, applications and services."[3]

Series3 features such as certification for home theater use, organic light-emitting diode (OLED) display on the front of the DVR, and more. The TiVo HD sold for approximately $300.

With Rogers working on sales, partnerships, and marketing, Ramsay kept focused on the vision for the company, the bigger picture. In 2007, in addition to his role as TiVo chairman of the board, Ramsay took a new position as a venture partner with the company New Enterprise Associates. He also served on the boards of a number of technology companies, including Ooma Inc., Loopt Inc., Netflix Inc., Conviva Inc., and Fanhattan Inc. While Ramsay shifted into new positions in and outside of TiVo, and Rogers excelled in his new role as CEO, Barton kept his roles as TiVo's CTO and the senior vice president of research and development. Leaving the day-to-day operations to Rogers seemed like it was going to work out well.

ANOTHER FALL

Although things were looking up for TiVo, it had been struggling to maintain its hold on the market ever since losing the partnership with DIRECTV. Hiring Rogers had helped stabilize the company, but some critics said TiVo was not as innovative or creative as it needed to be and wished the company would update the remote control or make applications available for portable devices. In addition, more and more cable companies started competing in the DVR market. Several DVR brands were now available to consumers. Cable companies started offering their own DVR packages for free as part of their service contracts. In 2008, TiVo again made the difficult decision to lay off staff in order to save money on salaries. The company had survived challenges before, though, and hoped it would survive this one.

In the midst of these struggles, TiVo was also busy defending its patents. In 2009, as litigation with EchoStar was still pending, TiVo filed additional patent infringement lawsuits

INFRINGEMENT PROTECTION

According to US Intellectual Property Enforcement Coordinator Victoria Espinel, "intellectual property are the ideas behind inventions, the artistry that goes into books and music, and the logos of companies whose brands we have come to trust."[4] The government has enacted laws to protect the inventors, creators, writers, and product designers of the world from having their ideas stolen and used by others for profit. Espinel believes "infringement of intellectual property can hurt our economy and can undermine US jobs. Infringement also reduces our markets overseas and hurts our ability to export our products."[5] Intellectual property law can be quite complicated, with whole schools dedicated to training people to practice this type of law. The three main types of protection for intellectual property are copyright, trademark, and patent protection.

against telecommunications giants Verizon and AT&T, claiming both were using technology TiVo had invented.

Several lawsuits were in process, the number of TiVo subscribers had declined, and the company's financial situation was on shaky ground, but TiVo weathered the storm. In a positive sweep in 2009, TiVo licensed its software to cable company Cox Communications, renewed its lucrative contract with Comcast, and reinitiated a relationship with DIRECTV. In late 2009, TiVo posted its first profitable fiscal year—ten years after the company began. +

Rogers faced many struggles at TiVo as CEO
after Ramsay stepped down.

In 2010, TiVo partnered with HP to revisit the original
home server idea from which it was born.

TIVO'S FUTURE

B y the late 2000s, TiVo had come full circle. In
addition to finally posting a profitable year,
it seemed a version of Barton and Ramsay's
original idea—the home server network—could
come to fruition. The technology that had not

existed in 1997 had started catching up to their vision. In 2010, TiVo partnered with Ramsay and Barton's early employer HP to develop a home server application, called the Windows Home Server add-in. The application enables users to store recorded TiVo content and transfer it to their computer, gaming system, and any other compatible device. Content can also be transferred back to the TiVo.

CONTINUED COLLABORATIONS

TiVo continued changing with the times and implementing new innovations. In March 2010, the TiVo Series4, in the form of the TiVo Premiere and TiVo Premiere XL, debuted. The Premiere versions have access to on-demand movies, television programs, and music for rent or purchase. The devices recorded up to 45 (Premiere) or

"We constantly think about how we can make it bigger. DVR is only one application of this platform. We've already expanded into home networking where you can get music and pictures from your PC and connect multiple cables together on the home network, so ultimately you're going to see content delivered to your TiVo over broadband. It doesn't just involve recording your favorite shows but will become a way for you to integrate and manage all your home entertainment and media. We want TiVo to become more important than a microwave, more important than a cell phone, but probably not more important than the TV, because we need one of them."[1]

—*Mike Ramsay on TiVo's future*

TiVo has continually sought new partnerships, integrating popular media platforms such as Netflix.

150 (Premiere XL) hours of HD programming or 400 and 1,350 hours of SD, respectively. The TiVo Premiere was updated March 2012 to provide up to 75 hours of HD programming and 640 hours of SD programming.

TiVo expanded its services to include partnerships with Internet radio company Pandora in September 2010. A partnership with Apple for an iPad app was made in January 2011. That same month, TiVo partnered with cell phone, television, and Internet company Virgin Media in the United Kingdom. In November, TiVo expanded further, launching a partnership with Spain's largest cable company, ONO. The ability for TiVo users to watch programs through online video on-demand services such as Hulu, YouTube, and Netflix also became available as of 2011.

In October of that year, the TiVo Premiere Elite was released. Recordable programming time was raised to 300 hours of HD or 2,200 hours of SD. The number of shows that can be recorded at one time also doubled. The newest generation TiVo now recorded four shows at once.

MORE LAWSUITS AND LEADERSHIP SHIFTS

In 2011, TiVo's lengthy lawsuit against EchoStar and Dish Network was settled. The lawsuit had been a legal tug-of-war between the companies. When it ended, Dish Network and former parent company EchoStar were ordered to pay TiVo a total sum of $500 million—$300 million up front and $200 million in six annual payments between 2012 and 2017. As part of the settlement, TiVo authorized Dish Network and EchoStar a license to use its technology.

DVRs AND COMMERCIALS COEXIST AFTER ALL

In 2011, independent consulting firm Deloitte noted that DVR technology would be present in more than 50 percent of television households by the end of 2011. By contrast, in 2006, only 17 percent of the homes in the United States had a DVR. While the growth is impressive, a huge portion of the market share is still up for grabs.

Deloitte claimed television advertising would go almost entirely unchanged despite the fact that DVRs would be in so many households. It was theoretically possible that all of the households with DVRs could skip commercials, but it did not seem to be the case that they were, according to the firm. Even though people had DVR technology, most viewers continued to watch "event television" such as major sporting events, awards shows, and news programs as they are broadcast live, to feel they are part of the event.[3] Commercial spots for sporting events such as the Super Bowl and World Series continue to sell for millions of dollars for less than a minute of airtime. In the view of Deloitte's consultants, in order for viewers to miss seeing commercials, they would have to either pre-record everything they watched on television or close their eyes. And neither of those things seemed likely, they concluded.

In March 2012, TiVo cofounder Barton resigned as CTO to pursue "his next big idea."[2] Barton did not cut ties with the company completely, but stayed on as a consultant for the lucrative sum of $25,000 a month. The consultant role would include weighing in on any patent and litigation and some technical matters. Barton's shift came the year after the massive EchoStar settlement and right on the heels of another win. A lawsuit against AT&T that had been filed in 2009 was settled in January 2012, mere weeks ahead of

Barton's departure. TiVo was awarded approximately $215 million from AT&T as a result of the aggressive defense TiVo had initiated. Some speculated keeping Barton as a consultant on litigation matters may have been influenced by the recent win against AT&T.

CONTINUED COMPETITION

Competition continued to be a challenge for TiVo as of 2012. Cable and satellite companies around the country often include DVR technology in contracts with consumers. TiVo continues enforcing its patents by taking to court companies that use TiVo technology without paying a licensing fee. Even though the companies' devices may not have the breadth of services TiVo offers, the convenience of renting a box from a satellite or cable company often outweighs the extra service fee and piece of equipment required to subscribe to TiVo.

Despite this, TiVo continues appealing to consumers as an easy-to-use, convenient machine, and appealing to advertisers by offering data collection, targeted advertising, pre-loaded ads, and the ability to add new commercials to stored data.

In early 2012, TiVo estimated that only 38 percent of their customers' viewing time is spent

As early as 2004, the online community speculated that the word TiVo might be entered into *Webster's New World College Dictionary* as a verb describing the action of recording live television. Because the company name is trademarked, it is technically a noun. Barton said "there's a particular . . . set of legal steps that we need to take to protect our trademark, to protect that verb, and so we have to take actual action to tell people that when they use TiVo as a verb, that you can't do that."[4] Despite this, as of 2012 *Merriam-Webster's Dictionary* lists it as a transitive verb meaning "to record (as a television program) with a DVR."[5] As more and more people use TiVo DVRs, using the brand name to describe the action has become quite common.

watching live television. People are using their TiVos to watch recorded shows nearly two-thirds of the time. This was exactly what TiVo hoped would happen since its start in 1997. TiVo did not bring about the death of commercial television as so many had feared. People are still exposed to commercials, and TiVo's continued ability to morph with the market by partnering with popular and innovative Internet services such as YouTube, Netflix, and Facebook has kept the company at the forefront of the DVR market. +

TiVo technology has a place in television history
and looks to be a part of its future as well.

TIMELINE

1950	1958	1972
Mike Ramsay is born in Scotland.	Jim Barton is born in the United States.	Ramsay graduates from Edinburgh University.

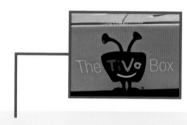

1999	1999	1999
The TiVo is unveiled at the Communications Electronic Show in Las Vegas, Nevada, in January.	The first TiVo DVR ships in March.	In September, TiVo makes an IPO (Initial Public Offering), selling its first shares of company stock to the public.

1980

Barton graduates from the University of Colorado at Boulder.

1997

Ramsay and Barton found their company Teleworld Inc. in August.

1998

Teleworld's name is changed to TiVo, and the logo is created in June.

2001

The FTC investigates TiVo as a result of a congressional request on privacy in May.

2001

The TiVo Series2 ships in December.

2003

Marty Yudkovitz is hired as president in May.

TIMELINE

2003

TiVo reaches its one-millionth subscriber in November.

2005

Ramsay steps down as CEO in January.

2005

In February, TiVo president Marty Yudkovitz announces he will step down.

2007

TiVo HD is released in July.

2009

TiVo posts its first profitable year.

2010

The TiVo Series4 devices, or TiVo Premiere and TiVo Premiere XL, debut in March.

2005	2006	2006
Tom Rogers starts as TiVo CEO in July.	TiVo wins a Primetime Emmy Award in July.	The TiVo Series3 is released in September.

2011	2011	2012
TiVo releases an app for the iPad in January.	The TiVo Premiere Elite debuts in March.	Barton steps down as CTO in March.

ESSENTIAL FACTS

CREATORS

Mike Ramsay (1950–)

Jim Barton (1958–)

DATE LAUNCHED

August 4, 1997 (Teleworld launched)

June 1998 (company changed to TiVo to represent refocused DVR idea)

CHALLENGES

As cofounders of TiVo, Mike Ramsay and Jim Barton overcame numerous challenges as they started their business. They had difficulty explaining an initial concept of the company to investors and then convincing consumers they needed the product that came from a refocused vision—the DVR. Once established, TiVo faced intense competition with other DVR makers, dealt with anger from television network and advertising executives, and fought to defend its patented technology.

SUCCESSES

Although it struggled gaining widespread acceptance upon its initial rollout, the TiVo soon developed a cultlike following. A feature allowing viewers to speed through commercials caused strain with television and advertising executives, but the TiVo team sought alternatives to appease executives. In comparison to a competing DVR that targeted and cut out commercials, the TiVo was a less renegade technology. TiVo gained acceptance and respect from executives, and remains at the top of the DVR market amongst many competitors.

IMPACT ON SOCIETY

The TiVo DVR, which records and pauses live television programming, was considered revolutionary upon its unveiling. Features allowing viewers to speed past commercials, record more than one program at a time, seek programs to record by keyword, and connect their TiVo with other technologies changed the way people watch television.

QUOTE

"When we started, we really thought about the kind of company we wanted to have, rather than the products we wanted to create. We wrote a list of core principles for our company to follow. One of them was 'It just works,' meaning everything has to work in the most fundamental, easy, intuitive way possible. The principles were strong from day one and set the tone for how our products were created and how we treated our employees."

—*Mike Ramsay*

GLOSSARY

architect
> A person who designs a Web site or program.

brand
> The identity of a product as defined by its name and trademark, logos, slogans, or public impression of a product.

capital
> The total wealth or worth, including combined cash, property, and stocks, that is owned by a company.

commercial television
> Television programs that are funded through the sales of advertising and which are often interrupted by those advertisements.

consumer
> Someone who uses and buys a product or service.

demographic
> A portion of the public that shares common characteristics such as age, living conditions, income, etc.

digital
> Involving or relating to the use of computer technology.

expertise
> High-level skill or knowledge in a certain area.

investor
> Someone who offers money to the benefit of a specific business project, with an expectation of sharing in the profits.

lucrative

Profitable or moneymaking.

memory

Where data and program information is stored on a computer for later retrieval and use.

modem

An electronic device that transmits data from one computer to another via phone lines.

monopoly

An organization that takes over and controls something, such as an industry.

network

A company that provides programming to be broadcast over radio and television stations.

philanthropist

A person who donates money to charitable organizations with the hope of helping others.

software

The programs used to direct the operations of a computer.

start-up

A young business enterprise.

ADDITIONAL RESOURCES

SELECTED BIBLIOGRAPHY

Coppa, Matt. "The Tao of TiVo: Wisdom from the Men Who Changed How the World Watches TV." *Men's Fitness.* May 2004: 78. Print.

Harris, Jessica. Interview with Jim Barton, cofounder of TiVo. *From Scratch: A Radio Show about the Entrepreneurial Life.* NPR. 23 Nov. 2011. Podcast. 25 Apr. 2012.

Lewis, Michael. "Boom Box." *New York Times Magazine.* 13 August 2000. Web. 14 Dec. 2011.

Livingston, Jessica. *Founders at Work: Stories of Startups' Early Days.* New York: Apress, 2007. Print.

FURTHER READINGS

Abrahamson, Albert, and Christopher H. Sterling. *The History of Television, 1942 to 2000.* Jefferson, NC: McFarland, 2003. Print.

Bellamo, Michael, and Todd W. Carter. *How to Do Everything with Your TiVo.* New York: McGraw-Hill/Osborne Media, 2004. Print.

WEB LINKS

To learn more about TiVo, visit ABDO Publishing Company online at **www.abdopublishing.com**. Web sites about TiVo are featured on our Book Links page. These links are routinely monitored and updated to provide the most current information available.

PLACES TO VISIT

Computer History Museum
1401 N Shoreline Blvd.
Mountain View, CA 94043
http://www.computerhistory.org
Visitors to the museum can tour informational displays complete with actual models and artifacts illustrating the history of computers and other revolutionary electronics. The museum houses several TiVo items as part of its collection, such as early manuals and remote controls.

Museum of Science and Industry
5700 Lake Shore Drive
Chicago, IL 60637
http://www.msichicago.org/
Interactive exhibits and tours let visitors explore the world of scientific discoveries and innovations. Hands-on displays and interesting artifacts teach the history and logistics of particular inventions, including a Smart Home exhibit that displays a TiVo Slide Remote.

SOURCE NOTES

CHAPTER 1. AN IDEA FORMS

1. Matt Haughley. "Seven Questions with Michael Cronan, Designer and Creator of the Name 'TiVo' and the Mascot." *PVRblog*. Matt Haughley, 7 Dec. 2005. Web. 25 Apr. 2012.

2. Michael Lewis. "Boom Box." *New York Times Magazine*. New York Times Company, 13 Aug. 2000. Web. 25 Apr. 2012.

3. Business Wire. "TiVo to Unveil 1999's Hottest Consumer Electronics Breakthrough at CES with First Public Demo of Personal Television." *Business Library*. CBS Interactive, 7 Jan. 1999. Web. 25 Apr. 2012.

4. Adrienne Faillace. "Blame it on Bulova: Commercial Television Turns 70!" *Archive of American Television*. Academy of Television Arts & Sciences Foundation, 30 June 2011. Web. 25 Apr. 2012.

CHAPTER 2. THE FOUNDERS

1. "Alumni News." *School of Engineering - Newsletter* (2007). University of Edinburgh, Dec. 2007. Web. 25 Apr. 2012.

2. Jessica Harris. Interview with Jim Barton, cofounder of TiVo. *From Scratch: A Radio Show about the Entrepreneurial Life*. NPR. 23 Nov. 2011. Podcast. 25 Apr. 2012.

CHAPTER 3. GETTING OFF THE GROUND

1. "TiVo Founder: 'Life is Too Short' (video)." *CNN Money*. Cable News Network, 6 July 2010. Web. 25 Apr. 2012

2. Jessica Harris. Interview with Jim Barton, cofounder of TiVo. *From Scratch: A Radio Show about the Entrepreneurial Life*. NPR. 23 Nov. 2011. Podcast. 25 Apr. 2012.

3. Jessica Livingston. *Founders at Work: Stories of Startups' Early Days*. New York: Apress, 2007. Print. 194.

4. Christine Y. Chen. "TiVo Is Smart TV (But Hey, Brains Aren't Everything). It Was Supposed to Change Everything: TV, Advertising, Even the Mass Market. So Why Isn't Wall Street Playing Along?" *CNN Money (Fortune)*. Cable News Network, 19 Mar. 2001. Web. 25 Apr. 2012.

5. Michael Lewis. "Boom Box." *New York Times Magazine*. New York Times Company. 13 Aug. 2000. Web. 25 Apr. 2012.

6. Jessica Harris. Interview with Jim Barton, cofounder of TiVo. *From Scratch: A Radio Show about the Entrepreneurial Life*. NPR. 23 Nov. 2011. Podcast. 25 Apr. 2012.

7. Jessica Livingston. *Founders at Work: Stories of Startups' Early Days*. New York: Apress, 2007. Print. 195.

CHAPTER 4. CREATING TIVO

1. Matt Coppa. "The Tao of TiVo." *Men's Fitness*. American Media, 7 May 2004. Web. 25 Apr. 2012.

2. Matt Haughley. "Seven Questions with Michael Cronan, Designer and Creator of the Name 'TiVo' and the Mascot." *PVRblog*. Matt Haughley, 7 Dec. 2005. Web. 25 Apr. 2012.

3. Ibid.

4. Jessica Loebig. "History." *TiVo*. TiVo, n.d. Web. 25 Apr. 2012.

5. Matt Coppa. "The Tao of TiVo." *Men's Fitness*. American Media, 7 May 2004. Web. 25 Apr. 2012.

6. Jessica Loebig. "History." *TiVo*. TiVo, n.d. Web. 25 Apr. 2012.

7. Jessica Livingston. *Founders at Work: Stories of Startups' Early Days*. New York: Apress, 2007. Print. 196.

CHAPTER 5. CONVINCING THE PUBLIC

1. Peter Rojas. "The Engadget Interview: Mike Ramsay, CEO of TiVo." *Engadget*. AOL, 18 Oct. 2004. Web. 25 Apr. 2012.

SOURCE NOTES CONTINUED

2. Matt Haughley. "Seven Questions with Michael Cronan, Designer and Creator of the Name 'TiVo' and the Mascot." *PVRblog*. Matt Haughley, 7 Dec. 2005. Web. 25 Apr. 2012.

3. Michael Lewis. "Boom Box." *New York Times Magazine*. New York Times Company. 13 Aug. 2000. Web. 25 Apr. 2012.

4. Peter Rojas. "The Engadget Interview: Mike Ramsay, CEO of TiVo." *Engadget*. AOL, 18 Oct. 2004. Web. 25 Apr. 2012.

5. Paul Grunwald. "TiVo Review." *Gadgeteer*. Gadgeteer. 10 Apr. 2001. Web. 25 Apr. 2012.

6. Laura A. Locke "TiVo." *Time Magazine*. Time, 7 July 2003. Web. 25 Apr. 2012.

7. Jessica Harris. Interview with Jim Barton, cofounder of TiVo. *From Scratch: A Radio Show about the Entrepreneurial Life*. NPR. 23 Nov. 2011. Podcast. 25 Apr. 2012.

CHAPTER 6. COMPETITORS, PARTNERS AND AN IPO

1. "Leadership: Paul G. Allen." *Vulcan*. Vulcan, n.d. Web. 25 Apr. 2012.

2. Jessica Livingston. *Founders at Work: Stories of Startups' Early Days*. New York: Apress, 2007. Print. 199.

3. "Strategies for Going Public." *Deloitte*. Deloitte, n.d. Web. 25 Apr. 2012.

4. Jessica Livingston. *Founders at Work: Stories of Startups' Early Days*. New York: Apress, 2007. Print. 199.

CHAPTER 7. SURVIVING

1. Robert Pitovsky. Letter to Edward J. Markey. Department of Computer Science at University of Massachusetts Lowell, 11 May 2001. PDF File. 20 Dec. 2011.

2. Ibid.

3. Jessica Livingston. *Founders at Work: Stories of Startups' Early Days*. New York: Apress, 2007. Print. 199, 202.

CHAPTER 8. DARK DAYS

1. Molly Wood. "A Conversation with TiVo CEO Tom Rogers (video)." *CNET*. CBS Interactive, 15 Apr. 2010. Web. 25 Apr. 2012.

2. Ibid.

3. Krista Wierzbicki. "TiVo Awarded 2006 Interactive Television Emmy." *TiVo*. TiVo, 27 July 2006. Web. 25 Apr. 2012.

4. Victoria Espinel. "About the Office of the U.S. Intellectual Property Enforcement Coordinator (IPEC)." *The White House President Barack Obama*. White House, n.d. Web. 25 Apr. 2012.

5. Ibid.

CHAPTER 9. TIVO'S FUTURE

1. Matt Coppa. "The Tao of TiVo." *Men's Fitness*. American Media, 7 May 2004. Web. 25 Apr. 2012.

2. Edward Moyer. "TiVo Co-founder and CTO Jim Barton Steps Down." *CNET*. CBS Interactive, 17 Mar. 2012. Web. 25 Apr. 2012.

3. Deloitte. "DVRs Proliferate! The 30 Second Spot Doesn't Die!" *Deloitte*. Deloitte, 18 Jan. 2011. Web. 25 Apr. 2012.

4. Jessica Harris. Interview with Jim Barton, cofounder of TiVo. *From Scratch: A Radio Show about the Entrepreneurial Life*. NPR. 23 Nov. 2011. Podcast. 25 Apr. 2012.

5. "TiVo." *Merriam-Webster*. Merriam-Webster, n.d. Web. 25 Apr. 2012.

INDEX

ABOUT THE AUTHOR

Kristine Carlson Asselin is the author of close to a dozen children's books for the school library and elementary markets. In addition to nonfiction, she writes Young Adult and Middle Grade fiction. She has a bachelor of science degree from Fitchburg State University and an master of arts degree from the University of Connecticut. A member of the Society of Children's Book Writers and Illustrators (SCBWI), Asselin loves attending workshops to practice her craft and meet other writers. Asselin lives with her husband and daughter in a suburb near Boston.

PHOTO CREDITS